Squeaky Cheese

Squeaky Cheese

The Ultimate Guide to Making Finnish Leipäjuusto

Susan Raisanen

Squeaky Cheese: The Ultimate Guide to Making Finnish Leipäjuusto

Copyright © 2016 by Susan Raisanen

ISBN 978-0-9889473-8-2

Published by The Arizona Marketing Association, Scottsdale, AZ

All rights reserved. No part of this book may be used or reproduced by any means, graphic, electronic, or mechanical, including photocopying, recording, taping, or by any information storage retrieval system without the written permission of the author except in the case of brief quotations embodied in critical articles and reviews.

Cover painting by Lavona Keskey.

Printed in the United States of America.

In loving memory of my mother, Millie Raisanen, and my grandmother, Mary Raisanen. Grandma is the one who taught Mom how to make juusto back in the early 1950s when she moved from White Bear Lake to the farm.

This one is for you, Dad. It was perhaps your love of our Finnish heritage and all those stories you told that created that same interest and love for roots in me.

Many thanks to the thousands of people who have watched, and the hundreds of you who have sent such nice messages after watching the YouTube video I put up a little over a year ago. Wow! I knew some people would be interested in knowing how to make this lovely cheese, but I never had any idea of HOW many.

Carrying on Traditions

Table of Contents

Foreword..	xiii
Esipuhe: (Foreword in Finnish)................	xv
Our Background: Pioneer Lane Farm..........	3
Getting Started: Here's What You'll Need....	7
Let's Do It!: Directions............................	11
How to Eat It: Serving Hints....................	23
Finnish Squeaky Cheese Recipe................	25
About the Author...................................	27
Cokato FAHS.......................................	29

Foreword

Squeaky Cheese, that delicious, traditional delicacy from your mothers of ages past.

In the Swiss Alps during the time the cows were in pasture, the shepherds prepared delicious cheese from the milk of their cows when there was no cool storage. The Greeks cultured their milk into yogurt and prepared Feta cheese. The French monks forgot their cheese in the caves and, as a result, Roquefort cheese was born. The Finnish mothers from ages past baked their milk into Squeaky cheese, a simple, but tasty delicacy during the time when their only cold storage was outside in the bone-chilling cold.

In the northeast part of Finland, Taivalkoski, at the Juusola house near the end of the 1800s, the matriarch of the house taught the secrets of cheesemaking to her daughter Mary. The house was large for that time in Finland. The building was 46 yards long. They had close to 50 people among the four families dwelling there. There were around 20 cows which, besides providing enough milk for drinking at mealtimes and making butter, there was enough for cheesemaking. Just as  her brother and sister had done, Mary was planning to move to the United States to Minnesota to work as a housemaid. Her mother, Anna, wanted the skills of a good homemaker to go with Mary into the big world.

Going visiting and as a gift to relatives, you would prepare cheese. Likewise, each respectable homemaker made cheese for the weekend to be served with coffee. Mary's nephew, Toivo, related that in the 1940s, it was customary for their family to make cheese for each family member during haying season. Beginning around the 1990s, in that same house and in that same great room, I was able to

Foreword

bake that traditional squeaky cheese and serve it to my relatives that came to visit from across the ocean.

Susan, with her parents and siblings were pleasant and beloved guests when they came to greet their relatives at the home where Mary, Susan's paternal grandmother was born. We talked about the old Finnish ways, stories flew through the air, and history came alive as we were digging in the buildings that were built in the 1600-1800s, and we became familiar with the old traditions as we looked at them through the eyes of a person in the year 2000. Susan watched when I prepared the squeaky cheese, just as her grandmother Mary had done, in the same traditional way as many, many generations before us had done. There was a warmth and a closeness felt at the respectfulness in which Susan was following the unbroken chain of the Finnish traditional work and skill that had been passed for centuries from mother to daughter.

Certainly in modern Finland, Squeaky cheese is prepared in factories, and it is available at every supermarket. Of course, Squeaky cheese tastes best when it is homemade, and shared in the company of good friends, with smiles and laughter around the coffee table!! And a suggestion would be to drink the coffee according to the Finnish tradition, with the cheese in the bottom of the coffee cup. Add coffee and a little bit of sugar. Always have at least two, if not three, small cups of coffee, and at the end you can enjoy and eat the warm, soft pieces of cheese. Certainly cheese is good served with fruit preserves as a dessert and is also used in salads.

I have been able to be one link in the chain of Finnish traditions, as I prepared and served homemade Squeaky cheese to my friends. With joy I have watched how Susan values and honors her Finnish roots, and one strong and concrete proof is the book you are holding. Squeaky cheese, a unique Finnish traditional delicacy, is now updated to today's standards and tastes. Thank you, Susan, for the work that you have done in preserving Finnish tradition.

Tasting good cheese and coffee, and hearing you laugh...

Your friend, Outi Alapirtti

Esipuhe

Leipäjuusto, tuo Suomalaisten esiäitien ajoilta periytyvä herkku. Sveitsin Alpeilla paimenet valmistavat laidunkaudella lehmiensä maidosta herkullisia juustoja kun vuoristossa ei ollut kylmäsäilytysmahdollisuutta. Kreikkalaiset hapattavat maidon jogurtiksi ja valmistavat fetaa. Ranskan munkit unohtivat juustonsa luoliin ja syntyi Roquefort. Suomalaiset esiäidit paistoivat maitonsa Leipäjuustoksi, yksinkertaiseksi, mutta maittavaksi herkuksi, aikana jolloin ainut kylmäsäilytys oli ulkona paukkuva hyytävä pakkanen.

Suomen koillisessa osassa Taivalkoskella, Juusolan talossa 1800- luvun lopulla talon emäntä opetti leipäjuuston teon salat tyttärelleen Marialle. Talo oli suuri sen aikaisessa Suomessa, rakennuksella mittaa 42 m ja asukkaitakin neljässä perhekunnassa lähemmäs 50. Lehmiä oli parisenkymmentä, joten maitoa riitti ruokajuoman ja voinvalmistuksen lisäksi myös juustonpaistoon. Kuten hänen veljensä ja siskonsa jälkiä  seuraten Maria oli muuttamassa Minnesotaan USAhan. Äiti-Anna tahtoi hyvän perheenemännän taitojen siirtyvän Marian mukana maailmalle.

Kyläilemään lähtiessä ja viemiseksi sukulaisille valmistettiin juusto. Samoin jokainen itseään kunnioittava perheenemäntä teki juuston viikonlopuksi tarjottavaksi kahvipöydässä. Kertoipa Marian veljenpoika Toivo, että 1940- luvulla oli heidän perheessään tapana heinäntekoaikaan tehdä oma juusto jokaiselle perheenjäsenelle. Tuossa samassa talossa, 1990-2000 luvulla, samassa isossa tuvassa minä sain paistaa perinteikästä leipäjuustoa ja tarjota sitä vierailulle merten takaa saapuville sukulaisilleni.

Esipuhe

Susan, vanhempiensa ja sisarustensa kanssa olivat mieluisat ja rakastetut vieraat käydessään tervehtimässä sukulaisiaan Susanin isän Paulin, äidin syntymäkodissa. Juttelimme vanhoista suomalaisista perinteistä, esineet ja tarinat leijailivat ilmassa kun kolusimme 1600- 1800 luvilla rakennettuja rakennuksia ja tutustuimme vanhoihin perinteisiin 2000-luvun ihmisen silmin. Susan seurasi isoäitinsä Marian tavoin, kun valmistin samalla perinteisellä tavalla leipäjuustoa kuin monet, monet sukupolvet meitä aikaisemmin. Lämpö ja läheisyys oli aistittavissa siinä kunnioituksessa jolla Susan seurasi katkeamatonta suomalaista perinnetyötä- taitoa joka on siirtynyt vuosisatoja äidiltä tyttärelle. Toki nykysuomessa juustoa valmistetaan teollisesti ja sitä on saatavilla jokaisen supermarketin valikoimasta. Mutta parhaaltahan leipäjuusto maistuu kuitenkin itsetehtynä ja hyvien ystävien kanssa hymyssä suin kahvipöydässä nautittuna!! Ja muistattehan juoda kahvin perinteiseen suomalaiseen tapaan? Juustoa pieninä palasina kahvikupin pohjalle, päälle kahvia ja hivenen sokeria. Kahvia juodaan ainakin kaksi ellei kolmekin pientä kupillista, ja sitten lopuksi syödään lämpimät, pehmennet juustopalat nautiskellen. Tokihan juusto on hyvää myös hillon kanssa jälkiruokana ja myös erilaisissa ruokaisissa salaateissa.

Olen saanut olla yksi linkki suomalaisen perinteen ketjussa valmistaessani ja tarjoillessani kotona tehtyä leipäjuustoa ystävilleni. Olen ilolla seurannut Susanin arvostusta ja kunnioitusta suomalaisiin juuriinsa – yhtenä vahvana konkreettisena tekona käsissänne oleva kirja. Leipäjuusto, ainutlaatuinen suomalainen perinneherkku, nyt päivitettynä tähän päivään ja tämän ajan ihmisten makumaailmaan. Kiitos Susan, siitä työstä jonka olet tehnyt suomalaisen perinteen säilyttämisen hyväksi!

Hyvän juustokahvin maun suussa tuntien, naurusi korvissani kuullen,

ystäväsi Outi Alapirtti

Introduction

Why Finnish Squeaky Cheese?

As a young girl one of the many warm memories of life on our farm, Pioneer Lane Farm, is of my mom making Finnish cheese. This was no ordinary cheese, but a very special treat. My dad was a Guernsey farmer, and I'm quite certain that the combination of Mom's recipe and the sweet milk from Dad's Guernseys is what made for a perfect pan of Finnish cheese.

Since this Finnish Squeaky cheese or juusto (pronounced you'-stow) was something that we had around at all times, whether fresh or frozen, I did not realize the novelty of it. I had no idea that most people had never heard of it, much less tasted it. Even for many of my friends with a Finnish heritage, juusto was a special treat they got only when going to company's house.

> *Finnish cheese or juusto, pronounced you-stow.*

It was after being away from home that I realized that this cheese was indeed something very special. Not only did it bring warm memories of the busy kitchen and the five gallon bucket of milk warming in the kitchen sink on Saturday mornings, but also a realization that Finnish cheese was not something that could be easily bought anywhere or made by just anybody!

After quite a few years away from home, I finally decided to take time to learn how to make cheese, this Finnish Squeaky Cheese, so that I could carry and pass the tradition to others.

Even though I had seen cheese made hundreds of times, I did not really pay attention so I needed to get very clear on it. Over the next few days, I made about five phone calls to Mom and a couple calls to my sisters until I knew perfectly well what to do, or so I thought. Even then, I finally had to just sit down and write the instructions exactly as Mom told me over the phone because it was not turning out quite right. That first week I made this juusto SIX times just to try perfect it! Yes, that's right, SIX times in one week!

That's when I decided to make a video showing the entire process. I knew that if I did not know how to do it even after watching the process so many times around home, others would surely be just as lost as I was.

At that time, I did not do much with the video other than sell a few copies of it. But then one day several years later, one of my good friends, Sinikka, a Finnish immigrant, said to put it up.

Little did I know that once the video went up, thousands and thousands of people would view it!

Because of all the feedback and messages I received, this book was born. It was time to just put it all in writing again.

Why Finnish Squeaky Cheese? Because we are carrying on traditions.

Our Background

Pioneer Lane Farm

It is always fun to stroll down Memory Lane to reminisce and remember old times, old friends, and old customs. Often, tied along with those memories of people and places, are the thoughts of certain foods. In fact, if we think hard enough, we can even taste or smell it!

Maybe it is something you remember from times spent at Grandma's and Grandpa's, or certain holidays spent with aunts and uncles, or other relatives and friends. Perhaps it was some of life's big events such as baptisms, confirmations, graduations, and weddings.

As is often the case, those celebrations included traditions and foods that were passed down through the generations, and for some of us, the traditions came from the land of our forefathers not too far back in our family history.

In this case, this one comes to you from Finland, from my grandmother on Dad's side, and then my mother.

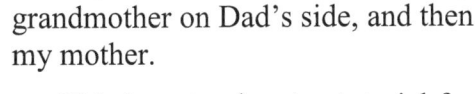

This is a step-by-step tutorial for making leipäjuusto, or more affectionately known as Squeaky Cheese. Finnish Squeaky Cheese.

Perhaps you are of Finnish heritage or maybe you are just curious what this is all about. Whatever the reason, you are in for a real treat, and it is my pleasure to share this deeply rooted traditional delicacy with you.

Just to give you an idea of where I came from. Here's Minnesota, and our family lived about 40 miles west of Minneapolis.

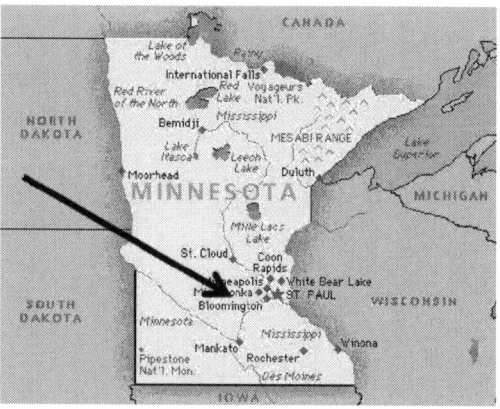

Our home was Pioneer Lane Farm, this place with an historical old round barn which had the best hayloft and the rope swings and lots of place to roam and have fun while growing up on this working dairy farm. The barn was built in 1901. Its diameter was 80 feet, and it measured 80 feet to the top of the cupola.

Our huge old house was built in 1917. It has three stories and a basement, and lots of beautiful oak woodwork. If the walls could tell the stories of all the people who lived and visited there, they would still be talking. Between family, guests and hired hands, there was seldom a dull moment on the farm.

Here are my parents. The years were good to them, and they were able to enjoy long life. They were still young at heart, even after a lifetime of hard work from sunup to sundown, farming and raising a big family.

All of their parents came from Finland. Dad's parents were from Kuusamo and Taivalkoski, and Mom's parents were from Kivijärvi and Ylitornio. Naturally, the Finnish culture was very near and dear to our family in many ways, of course because we had close ties to many relatives and friends over there.

My dad raised Guernseys. Guernseys are known for their high butter fat and high protein milk. With all that milk, there was enough to drink all we wanted and do all the baking we needed. My mom was an excellent cook, and had an abundant supply to make her cheese, too, the same recipe that was passed down the generations which started so long ago in Taivalkoski, Finland.

Squeaky Cheese, that Finnish delicacy, was something both of their mothers made, and it ended up becoming something that my mom became known for.

5

The secrets of cheesemaking have been passed on to us children and grandchildren, and now to you.

So now, let's get on to how to make it!

> "Squeaky Cheese played a part of my childhood. Whenever I went to the farm it was quite certain that my stay would also include eating supper there. And supper certainly included Squeaky Cheese, or at least that was my hope.
>
> The table was long and the chairs were many. I was just a child, and my eyes carefully watched as each item was brought from the kitchen to the dining room and handed to the nearest person to be passed around the table.
>
> The plate of cheese! How many little squares of that squeaky goodness were there compared to the number of people at the table? Would it be polite for me to take two or three pieces when the plate came to me? Did I dare?"
>
> Connie Aho, Phoenix, AZ

Getting Started

Here's What You Will Need:

Ingredients:

2 gallons of skim or raw milk. Do not use Whole Pasteurized milk. Whole Pasteurized Milk will not work. Raw milk straight from the dairy will work great, and milk fresh from a cow is best! I do not have easy access to raw milk, so I almost always use Organic skim milk. Non-organic will work, too, but not the ultra-pasteurized.

1 pint of heavy whipping cream (Use the cream only if you use skim milk. If you use raw milk, you don't need the cream.)

1/2 cup sugar

Squeaky Cheese

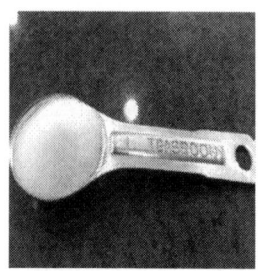

1 teaspoon salt

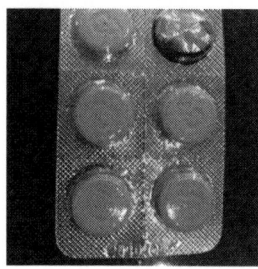

½ vegetable rennet tablet. I order rennet online from *www.cheesemaking.com*. If you do not have access to the internet or would rather call to order it, New England Cheesemaking Supply Company can be reached at **(413) 397-2012**. Just ask for their vegetable rennet tablets. You will get a whole pack. That is okay because they will keep for about 5 years in the freezer. Just keep them in the package they come and put that inside another freezer bag to store it.

Junket rennet tablets will NOT work for this! Don't try it. Trust me, I tried it and wasted the milk because it will not coagulate! I almost hate to admit this, but I could hardly believe it would not work, so I tried it again and wasted the milk twice! Your rennet must be cheesemaking rennet. Liquid vegetable rennet will work, too, and ½ of a tablet is the same as ½ teaspoon of liquid rennet.

> *J*unket rennet tablets will NOT work for this!

You will also need:

2 pans, 9 or 10 inch round is preferable, but 9 x 13 works well, too. I use the 9 x 13 from time to time, but I typically use the 9 inch round pan because I like my cheese a bit thicker than what you get in a 9 x 13.

Here's What You Will Need

A long stirring spoon that will reach the bottom of at least a 2 gallon bucket.

A 2-gallon bucket with a lid. Home Depot carries a really nice one that you can find in their paint supply section. Remember to get a lid, too. It's a little over 2 gallons, and it's very nice and sturdy. It works perfectly for cheese.

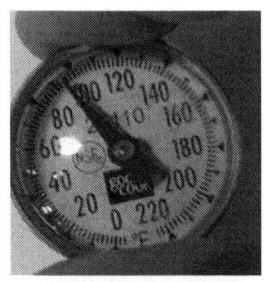

Meat thermometer. This thermometer needs to measure between 80 and 100 F degrees for sure, so a candy thermometer will not work.

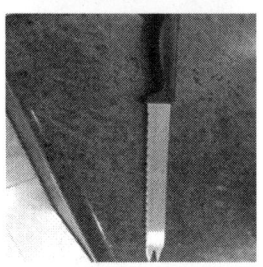

Long knife that will reach the depth of the 2-gallon bucket.

Tablespoon

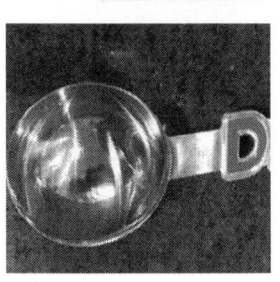

Squeaky Cheese

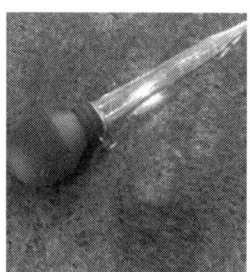 **Baster**

Time Required!

> *P*atience is a *V*irtue when making cheese. Your cheese will turn out best when you can let it sit as needed instead of rushing the process!

About 5 hours. Making cheese is something you cannot do when you are rushed. It is something that does not involve a whole lot of steps and something you can put going while you have other chores going on around the house. Even though it is not that complicated, it takes a long time for the curds and whey to separate. I say allow at least five hours and you'll be good.

You're ready!

Let's Do It!

Directions

First of all, you will need to warm your milk to anywhere from 96 to 98F degrees. What I usually do is one of two things. If I am going to be gone for the morning, I might just let the milk sit out on the counter for the morning, and then in the afternoon it will be at room temperature. Then I will warm it the rest of the way in the water bath. This seems to be a quicker way if you are not going to be home, and do not want the milk sitting in warm water all day.

Otherwise I just wash off the sides of the two gallons of milk, and put them right into a sink of hot water and let them warm up to lukewarm, but by no means, hot to the touch. Once the milk feels lukewarm to the touch, pour both of the gallons, (plus the cream, if you are using skim milk) into the 2-gallon bucket and cover. That covered 2-gallon bucket should soak in the hot water bath with water temperatures of 98 F degrees until the milk reaches that same temperature of 98 F degrees. Do not let your milk go over 98 F degrees.

After the milk has reached 96 – 98 F degrees, it is time to add the rest of the ingredients.

Water bath at 98 Degrees F.

At this time, take ½ of a rennet tablet and dissolve it in a tablespoon of lukewarm water. Just put a little bit of water in there, enough to dissolve it.

Set it aside while you add the next two ingredients.

Directions

Put in ½ cup sugar, and 1 teaspoon of salt. Stir the milk, sugar and salt mixture until you no longer feel the granules of salt and sugar in the bottom. That will take just a few minutes.

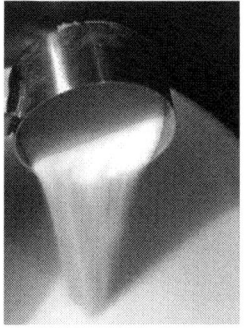 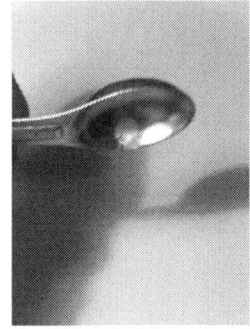 

Now just stir the rennet with a fork just a little bit to make sure it is dissolved in the tablespoon, and then pour it into the milk, sugar and salt mixture. Stir gently but well until the rennet has been distributed throughout.

 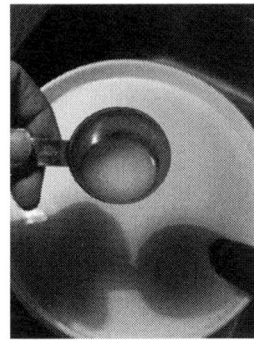 

Cover the bucket and let it sit for about 15 minutes. I usually also check the water and try keep it at an even 98 F degrees.

Try keep the water at or near 98 F degrees.

Squeaky Cheese

After 15 minutes of sitting, stir the mixture again VERY GENTLY, not fast, but very gently. Stir it to distribute the rennet, salt, and sugar evenly once again.

> *S*tir very gently.

Cover the bucket again, put it back in the water, and let it sit in the 98 F degree water for 45 to 60 minutes. I have found that an hour seems to work best, but different milk coagulates differently, so see what works best for you. It is better to sit too long than not long enough.

> *A*t this point, you have almost an hour to do other chores or visiting.

When you open the lid, it should have a jello-like texture. You can just press on it gently, and it should feel jelled.

Directions

Now take your long knife, one that will reach to the bottom of the bucket, and cut through the curds kind of like you are cutting a pizza. You are going to cut in 8 pieces all the way to the bottom.

Now take your long spoon and stir it gently, gently, gently until you no longer have any real large curds, and they have all been broken up. They should be larger than cottage cheese, but not huge. Maybe nickel-sized chunks.

Squeaky Cheese

Put the cover back on and let it sit in the 98 F degree water for another 45 minutes.

> *N*ow you have another 45 minutes to let it sit. Do you see why we say *P*atience is a *V*irtue?

When you open the cover now, you will see a pretty yellow whey at the top. You will get rid of the whey. It is sort of sweet and can be used in pancakes, bread or soup. If you have no use for it, just pour it out. By the time all is said and done, you will be getting rid of nearly a gallon and a half of whey!

Pour out what you can until the curds start threatening to come pouring out of the bucket. Then set the bucket back in the water and let it sit another 20 minutes or so. Pour out the extra whey. Repeat as often as necessary until you start to see only curds at the bottom.

> *P*our, Cover & Sit, Pour. *R*epeat as often as needed until most of the whey is gone.

Directions

Pour it out, let it sit, pour it out, let it sit. This is where you need patience, and patience really is a virtue if you want to make really good cheese. This part here is exactly why you need about five hours to make it!

Once you don't have that much whey left, you can either suction out the remaining whey with a baster, or pour the whey through a cheesecloth or very thin baking cloth. Just be careful not to mush up your curds or let them slip right down the drain.

Now you can pour the curds into your baking pan, and let it sit for about 20 minutes again. More whey will rise to the top. Simply baste it off again.

Let it sit again until you don't see much more whey.

Now take that cheese and flip it into the other pan. Put the exact same size pan on top, and flip it quickly while holding over the sink.

The reason you do this is because the curds flatten out nicely in the pan, and you will have a nice, flat roasting surface and the browning will be much more even.

Now that you have flipped the cheese, let it sit one more time for about 10 minutes and baste out the extra whey again.

> *Y*ou might want to take time out right now to put a pot of coffee going because your cheese is awfully close to being done! There is no doubt that warm cheese straight from the oven is the best!

You are ready to broil your cheese. Put the oven on Broil and put the rack at least one shelf higher than center so it is closer to the broiler, but not so close that it is within scorching distance.

Directions

Center your pan under the broiler so that it broils evenly. Keep the door partially open. DO NOT LEAVE the oven during this process. Once it starts to brown, it goes quickly! Stay close and keep a constant eye on it.

> *S*tay close and watch it!

Depending on your oven, you may need to rotate the pan in order to get certain areas of the cheese. Once the cheese is nicely and evenly browned around the whole surface of the cheese, remove it from the oven. Baste off the extra whey again.

Now take the other pan, and put it on top of the cheese. You are going to flip it, but pay close attention to the next instruction first!

Squeaky Cheese

> # *Pay Close Attention to This!*

You are going to flip the hot cheese over the sink and AWAY from you, not toward you because you do not want the hot liquid to splash in your face.

Flip it away from you very quickly, otherwise it will fold up in the pan and you will have a little bit of a mess in your pan because that cheese is hot and just kind of melts together. If it does happen to fold, though, no worries. Just jiggle the pan lightly and see if it starts to unfold on its own. Sometimes it will. If it does not, just use a large, thin spatula to help you unfold it nicely.

Now put it back in the oven and let the other side roast until it is nicely browned.

Remove the cheese from the oven and let it sit maybe 15 minutes so that it can settle and firm up a bit so that it does not lose its shape when you cut it.

Do not baste out the remaining liquid the last time. You do not want it to get too dry, so just let whatever is left of the whey sit in the pan with the cheese until it is cooled.

Once the cheese has cooled, keep it covered so it does not dry out.

Directions

There you have it; your first Finnish Squeaky Cheese!

> Grandma's Squeaky Cheese:
> You Might Eat a Whole Plate of It Before You Realize It!
>
> Molly Raisanen, Phoenix, AZ

How to Eat It

Serving Hints

It's best served warm, and it is delicious served with coffee. Just eat it in bite-sized chunks…

Or, if you want to do it the old Finnish way, you can put it in your coffee.

You can even serve this warm with whipped cream and berries or preserves on it. That's what some of the old Finns do.

This cheese also freezes very well. After it is cooled completely, cut it into four pieces and wrap them individually in Saran wrap or plastic wrap. Then put those wrapped pieces into another plastic freezer bag and lay them flat in the freezer.

This is a delicious treat to have on hand. It can be heated in the microwave. You can "zap" it for just a few seconds so it is a little bit warm. A great thing to have on hand for guests.

From Pioneer Lane Farm, enjoy a little taste of Finland.

I welcome your feedback. For those of you who are on Social Media, the hashtag is #FinnishCheese or #leipajuusto. Please share your pictures on Twitter! You can find me on Facebook, too. Just search for Susan Raisanen.

If you have any comments, questions or suggestions, please email me at susanraisanen@hotmail.com.

Enjoy your leipäjuusto, your Finnish Squeaky Cheese!

Finnish Squeaky Cheese

The Recipe

Ingredients:

2 gallons of skim or raw milk
1 pint of whipping cream
1/2 cup sugar
1 teaspoon salt
1/2 vegetable rennet tablet

You will also need:

2 pans, 9 or 10 inch round is preferable, but 9 x 13 works well, too.
A long stirring spoon
A 2-gallon bucket with a lid
Meat thermometer
Long knife that will reach the depth of the 2-gallon bucket
Tablespoon
Baster

Time Required:

About 5 hours

> *If you would like to see a video demonstration of this process, go to finnishcheese.com*

About the Author

Susan and her brothers and sisters were raised on Pioneer Lane Farm just West of Temperance Corner, the farm with the giant round barn and tall cupola that could be seen across the countryside.

In those years, the Raisanen family had a lot of touches of Finland in their ways and traditions. Her parents must have hosted hundreds of Finnish guests over the years. Susan was not fluent in the language at that time but had a keen interest in it, so while they were visiting she would sit in the living room with her Dad's Finnish-English dictionary and try to follow along the conversation.

After graduating from Dassel-Cokato High School in 1984, Susan spent a year as an exchange student in a Finnish Christian folk school, Jämsän kristillinen kansanopisto. During that year she studied and was able to get a pretty good grasp on the language, or enough so that she could communicate rather comfortably with the native people.

She also took classes in handwork and baking, and that is when she learned how to weave on those big, old looms and bake more of the traditional Finnish cuisine.

After returning to the USA, Susan attended college and became an elementary school teacher, and later went back to Finland to teach for two more years at Reisjärven kristillinen opisto. There she taught English, Finnish History, Piano, American Culture, and then translated classes for the North American students who were studying there. She and her students traveled the country many weekends putting on English Language & American Culture for various groups of people who called to ask.

During the three years Susan spent in Finland, she also visited the homes of all her grandparents. With the exception of her mother's father, who migrated as a youngster, all the rest were adults by the time they moved, and therefore had stories that had been told by them. In Susan's mind, it was especially nice to be able to come full circle, to the place where "her story" began.

The feeling Susan had when pulling into the driveway of her grandmother's home for the first time, the place and people she had heard so much about is nearly indescribable. The warmth of the people in the home definitely felt like the warmth of a family.

One of the best experiences Susan had while there was when her dad, Paul, came to Finland for the first time. There they explored family roots together, and it was especially touching and fun to be able to see him and his cousins meet after having spent a lifetime of communicating by letters. It was just as fun to go back a few years later with both her mom and dad!

Perhaps one of the biggest takeaways Susan had from her travels to Finland was a greater appreciation for what her grandparents gave up in order to cross that big ocean to the big "unknown". That desire was so strong they were willing to leave everything behind, even their families. It's hard to imagine. What guts and determination they had!

Susan Raisanen now resides in Scottsdale, Arizona, where she and two brothers own a software company, Profit Finder Pro Software. (www.ProfitFinderPro.com). There she works with business owners from across the United States, Canada and the United Kingdom, showing them how to use the software to help them pinpoint profit (or loss) points of their sales and marketing, and show what can be done to try turn those around. She has recently authored an Amazon bestseller book, "Track It To Crack It."

Although the distance is far, her love for Cokato and its people will never leave. The wind may blow and the leaves will flutter, but the roots hold strong. You know the saying, 'All hearts come home at Christmas"? It's true. Hearts come home more often than at Christmas, too!

Cokato Finnish-American Historical Society

We Remember So That Others Won't Forget.

Back in the early days of settlement around Cokato, many Finnish immigrants came to the area. Sometimes we wondered, "Why here when they could have chosen a beautiful beach or something like that?" They came because it was so similar to the land they left. They knew how to till the soil and farm the land. They knew how to work with the climate. They felt at home.

Cokato was not the first place for Finns to settle, but it is the place with the longest continuous settlement of Finns, now over 150 years.

In the late 1890s, the Onnen Toivo (Hope of Happiness) Temperance Society group built a Temperance Hall at the crossroads which later became known as Temperance Corner. The purpose was to provide opportunities to get together, socialize and have fun without alcohol. In later years, the one-room school was built and was in use until the early 1970s.

During the Winter War in Finland in the 1940s, this was a place where the locals would go to pack care packages to be sent to Finland. Many of their relatives or friends or just fellow Finns were living in very difficult circumstances, with little food and clothing.

During the 1970s and 80s when Susan was growing up, there were always activities at the corner during certain holidays, especially the Saturday of Memorial Day weekend. They usually biked up there to see what the old Finns were up to, and meet and chat with the locals.

Today the Cokato Finnish American Society has a very active group. People who grew up being active in the society with their parents are now taking over as they teach the next generations behind them. They demonstrate old crafts, give speeches and have a multitude of interesting ways to tell stories from the Old Country, the immigrants from the Old Country, and our history over and over again.

In their minds, "If we don't do it, who will?"

They are right. The Cokato Finnish American Historical Society. Carrying on traditions.

If you are interested in knowing more about the Cokato Finnish American Historical Society, go to www.cokatofinnam.org.

NOTES

NOTES

Printed in Great Britain
by Amazon